DISCOVERING THE APOSTLE ISLANDS

- HISTORY OF THE ISLANDS
- LIGHTHOUSE INFORMATION AND PHOTOS
- TRANSPORTATION INFORMATION
- RECOMMENDED ACTIVITIES AND PHOTO OPPORTUNITIES
- ISLAND DESCRIPTIONS/PHOTOS
- RECOMMENDED PLACES TO VISIT IN THE SURROUNDING COMMUNITIES

Discovering the Apostle Islands

Copyright © 2019 by Lawrence Newman

ISBN 978-0-9842918-3-0

Library of Congress Control Number: 2009911151

Printed in the United States of America

Sixth Edition

Publisher: Silver Millennium Publications, Inc.
Gold Canyon, Arizona

All rights reserved. No part of this book may be reproduced in any form, or by any means electronic, mechanical, recording, or otherwise, without written permission from the author, except for brief quotations used in reviews.

Front cover photo: Justice Bay, Sand Island

DISCOVERING THE APOSTLE ISLANDS

- ♦ WHERE TO GO
- ♦ WHAT TO DO
- ♦ HOW TO GET THERE

A VISITOR'S GUIDE
TO THE HISTORIC ISLANDS
OFF WISCONSIN'S NORTHERN SHORE

LAWRENCE NEWMAN

TO THE READER

After completing my first book "The Apostle Islands—America's Wilderness in the Water", which was written to serve as a handy pocket guide for the boater, kayaker, hiker, camper and beachcomber, it became apparent to me that a second book, one aimed at visitors coming to this beautiful area of Wisconsin, would also be useful.

Although visitors could make inquiries of local businesses and the local Chambers of Commerce, finding answers to many of their questions, it's possible that visitors might not be aware of many of the recreational opportunities available in the area, or have the time to discover them. It was with that thought in mind that this book was written.

I've been coming to this area of northern Wisconsin for over fifty years. My father was born in Ashland in 1909 and our family spent two-week vacations up here starting back in the early 1940's. I now spend much of the summer months in our home east of Ashland, which gives me the opportunity to continue to participate in many of the activities available in the area. In addition to a little fishing and boating in Chequamegon Bay I am able to do some sailing among the islands. I also visit the islands using the cruise service out of Bayfield.

In the pages that follow I have attempted to give the summer visitor to the Apostle Islands a quick overview of the activities available, and by an extensive collection of photographs, an appreciation of its beauty. I've also included my recommendations for places to visit on the mainland. There are many fine stores and restaurants that are worth your time, but space limitations prevented me from mentioning them all. The local Chambers of Commerce will provide information on many of these businesses.

I hope you can spend the time to visit and appreciate these beautiful historic islands and the surrounding area.

L. Newman
April 1, 2019

DISCOVERING THE APOSTLE ISLANDS

A VISITOR'S GUIDE TO THE HISTORIC ISLANDS OFF WISCONSIN'S NORTHERN SHORE

TABLE OF CONTENTS

General Comments—A Quick Overview.............. 1

A Brief History of the Islands……..…..………… 6

Getting to the islands:
   By cruise boat/ferry/water taxi......................... 10
   By sailboat…... 12
   By powerboat.. 13
   By kayak….. 15
   Charter fishing... 15
   Float plans... 15

Bayfield—Gateway to the Apostles..................... 16

Madeline Island…... 25

Stockton Island... 31

Raspberry Island... 35

Long Island and Chequamegon Bay.................... 39

Other Islands:
   Basswood….. 41
   Bear….. 43

Cat………………………………………………	45
Devils………………………………………..	48
Eagle………………………………………..	54
Gull…………………………………………..	55
Hermit……………………………………….	56
Ironwood……………………………………	57
Manitou……………………………………..	58
Michigan……………………………………	60
North Twin…………………………………	62
Oak…………………………………………..	64
Otter…………………………………………	66
Outer………………………………………...	67
Rocky……………………………………….	70
Sand…………………………………………	71
South Twin…………………………………	74
York………………………………………….	75
Recommended Activities………………….	77
Lighthouses…………………………………..	79
Major Beaches……………..……………….	86
Beach Stones……………………………….	89
Surrounding Communities:	
Ashland…………………………………….	91
Cornucopia………………………………...	95
Red Cliff……………………………………	96
Washburn………………………………….	97

Sources for Additional Information:
- Apostle Islands... 98
- Area Information.. 99
- Big Top Chautauqua..................................... 100
- Boating Regulations..................................... 100
- Camping—National Lakeshore....................... 100
- Campgrounds... 100
- Cruise Boat/Ferry/Water Taxi......................... 102
- Fishing Charters... 103
- Friends of the Apostle Islands National Lakeshore/Apostle Islands Historic Preservation Conservancy.......................... 104
- Golf Courses.. 104
- Hiking.. 105
- Kayaks/Canoes... 105
- Lighthouses... 106
- Museums... 107
- National Park Service................................... 108
- Northern Great Lakes Visitor Center.............. 108
- Sailboat Charters—Bareboat.......................... 108
- Sailboat Charters—Captained........................ 109
- Sailing Schools... 110

Thanks and Acknowledgments.......................... 112

Author Profile.. 113

GENERAL COMMENTS— A QUICK OVERVIEW

Unless travelers coming to the Apostle Islands area have done a considerable amount of preparation and planning beforehand, they are confronted with the problem of determining where the scenic spots in the islands are, and how to get to them. Obviously the time available to visit the islands is the determining factor as to what can be seen. With that in mind, recommendations for visit times of various lengths are presented below.

ONE DAY VISIT OPTIONS: (1) The three hour cruise by the tour boat service that operates out of Bayfield daily, mid-May to mid-October, gives the visitor a good feel for the beauty of the islands and, depending on wave and wind conditions, a close view of one of the Apostle Islands most scenic spots—the Devils Island sea caves. (2) For those visitors wishing a more physical experience, the two mile hike around Presque Isle Point on Stockton Island (Anderson Point Trail) is recommended to get "up close and personal" to the rugged beauty of an Apostle Island's shore. There is a tour boat trip to Stockton Island on Tuesdays and weekends, July 1st to Labor Day, with sufficient time to make the hike. (3) For those interested in visiting one of the most beautiful lighthouses in the islands, a trip to the Raspberry Island lighthouse is recommended. There is also a tour boat trip to this island on Tuesdays and weekends. July 1st to Labor Day   (4) A trip to Madeline Island can usually be accomplished at the visitor's convenience before or after experiencing one of the first three options. Cars can be transported on the ferry for an additional charge, allowing visitors to drive around the island. Mopeds and bicycles can be rented in La Pointe on Madeline Island.

TWO-DAY VISIT OPTIONS: (1) Any of the options shown above spread over two days. (2) A camping experience on Stockton Island (3) A sailing experience on one of the captained sailboats (4) A charter fishing experience (5) A kayaking excursion into the islands

LONGER VISITS: (1) All of the options noted above plus, depending on the visitor's preferences and time of his or her visit, the following activities. (2) A camping experience on one of the other, more remote, islands (3) If visiting in early September, trips to other island lighthouses by the cruise service, as part of the annual Lighthouse Celebration (4) Sailboat charters, either bareboat or captained (5) Individual power boating

All of the options listed above are described in the pages that follow. Be sure to contact the cruise service for other boat tours that may be available during your visit to the area.

CAMPING/DOCKING IN THE NATIONAL LAKESHORE: Camping in the National Lakeshore requires a permit that can be purchased at the Apostle Islands National Lakeshore Headquarters in Bayfield or at their office in Little Sand Bay. A discount priced block of six overnight docking tickets can be obtained in Bayfield, although the National Park Service primarily relies on self-registration by boaters using the docks for overnight stays. Collection stations consisting of steel boxes and envelopes are located on the islands having public docks.

AN OVERVIEW OF THE ISLANDS

The table below gives the approximate acreage and dimensions of the islands, and camping and public hiking trails availability. The map of the Apostle Islands that follows this table shows the position of the islands and proximity to the mainland.

ISLAND	SIZE IN ACRES	LNGTH/WDTH IN MILES	HIKING/ CAMPING
BASSWOOD	1,900	3-1/2 X 1-1/4	YES/YES
BEAR	1,800	2-1/4 X 1-3/4	NO/YES
CAT	1,300	3 X 1	NO/YES
DEVILS	300	1-1/4 X ½	YES/YES
EAGLE	28	½ X ¼	NO/NO
GULL	3	40YDSX250YDS	NO/NO
HERMIT	800	2 X ¾	NO/YES
IRONWOOD	700	1-1/4 X 1	NO/YES
LONG	300	3-1/2 X ¼	YES/YES
MADELINE	15,000	14 X 3	YES/YES
MANITOU	1,400	2-1/2 X 1	YES/YES
MICHIGAN	1,600	3-1/2 X 1-1/4	YES/YES
NORTH TWIN	200	1-1/4 X ¼	NO/YES
OAK	5,000	4 X 3	YES/YES

ISLAND	SIZE IN ACRES	LNGTH/WDTH IN MILES	HIKING/ CAMPING
OTTER	1,300	2 X 1-1/2	YES/YES
OUTER	8,000	6-1/4 X 2-1/2	YES/YES
RASPBERRY	300	1 X ½	YES/YES
ROCKY	1,100	2 X 1	YES/YES
SAND	2,900	3 X 3	YES/YES
SOUTH TWIN	400	1 X ¾	YES/YES
STOCKTON	10,000	7-1/4 X 2-1/2	YES/YES
YORK	300	1-1/2 X 3/4	NO/YES

Ticks and mosquitoes are common in the islands. Be sure to bring a good insect repellant.

Several of the islands have "zone" camping, instead of campsites. Areas have been set aside for remote backcountry camping on these islands. Contact the park service for additional information.

THE APOSTLE ISLANDS

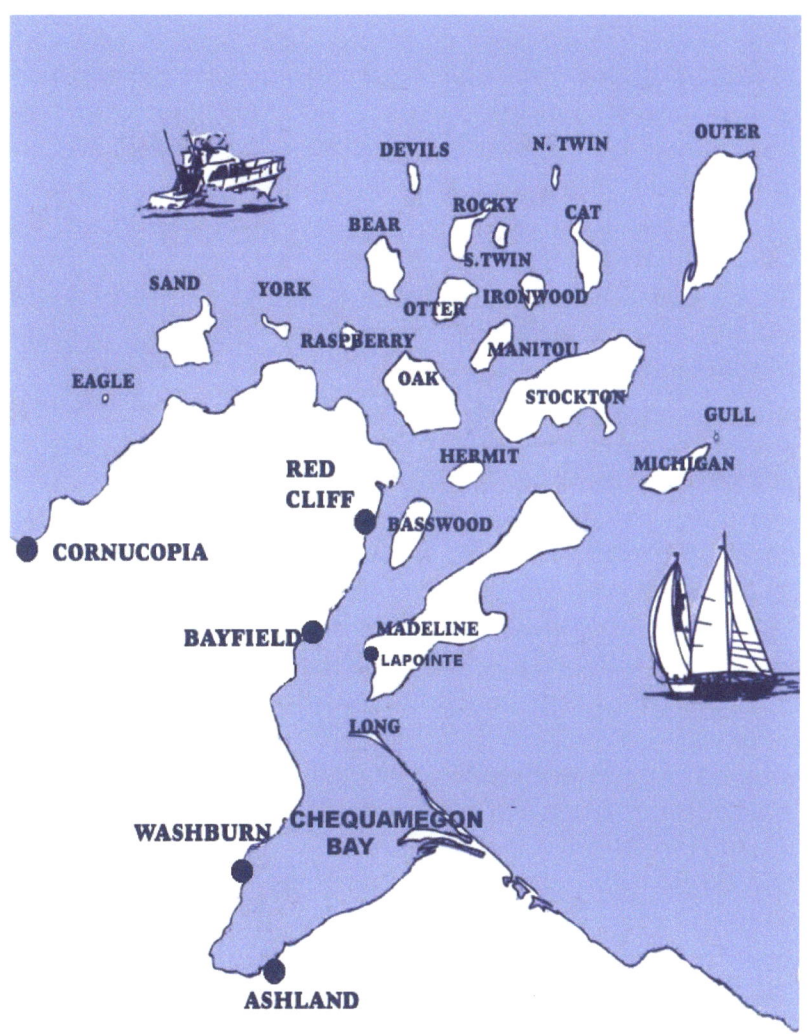

BRIEF HISTORY OF THE ISLANDS

The Apostle Islands, covering 720 square miles of western Lake Superior off Wisconsin's northern shore, were sculpted from 600 million year old sandstone by a series of glaciers that arrived around 2-½ million years ago and receded in the final period of glaciation about 10,000 years ago. Most of the beautiful beach stones, cobbles and boulders found along the shores of the islands were carried by the glaciers hundreds of miles and dropped as the glaciers melted.

There is some evidence dating back thousands of years that humans inhabited the area, not long after the glaciers receded. More recently, Native American oral histories indicate that the Ojibwe (Chippewa) migrated from the east to the Apostle Islands area about the time that Christopher Columbus sailed for the New World. Other Indian tribes were also active in the area including the Sioux, Huron, Fox and Ottawa.

During an active exploratory period French voyageurs established trade routes for their fur trading activities along the Great Lakes, including a portage route up the Brule River to connect with the Mississippi. The French lost political control to the British in 1762 after the French and Indian War. Subsequently, the area became part of the United States after the War of 1812.

Following a comparatively quiet period, the islands and the surrounding area were involved in extensive development of its natural resources. This was aided by immigrants from Northern Europe, beginning in the mid-1800s, close on the heels of the opening of the Sault Ste. Marie locks at the eastern end of Lake Superior and the arrival of the railroad. In addition to the expanded commercial fishing in the area, there was intensive lumbering in the islands and the surrounding mainland. Most of the islands were harvested for their lumber more than once. Lumber mills sprang up in the Bayfield area and along Chequamegon Bay. The quarrying of high quality brownstone from the islands and the mainland provided building material for many of the large Midwestern cities. A prime example of this brownstone construction can be found in the building housing the Apostle Islands National Lakeshore Headquarters in Bayfield, which was built using rock quarried from Basswood Island.

The shipment of iron ore bound for Chicago area steel mills from mines near Ashland was an enormous undertaking. Long trains carried ore to several docks in Ashland where it was loaded onto huge ore carriers, some more than two football fields in length. There were over twenty active mines supplying ore to the Ashland docks in 1892. The DuPont Corporation built one of the largest TNT production facilities in the United States on Chequamegon Bay, providing significant quantities of the explosives for munitions used in both World Wars and for land clearance, mining and quarrying in the area. Ashland also was a major distribution point for Eastern coal. Even with the bustling commercial activity in the region tourists came to the islands to escape the heat in the Midwestern cities and to view the raw beauty of the area.

During the mid-1890s the Chequamegon Bay region was the second busiest shipping area in the western Great Lakes, surpassed only by Chicago. It shipped nearly twice the tonnage of Milwaukee, Duluth and Superior combined. The commercial boom of this period ended very quickly.

By the mid-20th century, the commercial fishing industry had collapsed due to overfishing and the depredation of the sea lamprey brought about by the construction of the Welland Canal around Niagara Falls. Brownstone quarrying ended much earlier due to new construction methods involving steel. Today's overgrown quarry sites contain brownstone blocks ready for shipping that lay were they were on the last working day. The quality of the iron ore taken from the Gogebic Range, east of Ashland, was no longer economically viable for iron production, resulting in the closing of the mines and the Ashland ore docks. Subsequently, the railroads that had carried the ore discontinued all service into the area. The large stands of lumber were gone and lumbering operations moved on to other areas to the north and west. The TNT plant drastically phased down operations after World War II and finally closed. Open pit mining in the West eliminated the need for Eastern coal distribution through Ashland. In a comparatively short number of years the area became what it is today. Only the tourists kept coming—and in greater numbers.

Following several attempts to make the area a national park starting in 1930, Congressional hearings were held in 1967 and 1969. President Nixon signed the bill establishing the Apostle Islands National Lakeshore on September 26, 1970.

There are 22 Apostle Islands of which 21 are included in the Apostle Islands National Lakeshore. Only Madeline Island was not included due to the extensive residential and commercial development on the island when the national park was formed in 1970. In addition, a twelve-mile section of the mainland south of Sand Island was included in the park. Originally there were 20 islands in the park; Long Island was added in 1986. Some areas on Rocky and Sand Islands are still under life leases granted by the Park Service to the original owners.

Although there is some disagreement as to how the islands got their name, the most widely circulated belief on this subject is that the early missionaries to the area believed, or chose to believe, there were only twelve islands.

GETTING TO THE ISLANDS

BY CRUISE BOAT/FERRY/WATER TAXI

For the short-term visitor the principal method to gain access to the islands is the cruise boat service. The cruises described below leave from the city dock at the foot of Rittenhouse Avenue in Bayfield or from the dock just north of the city dock. Tickets can be ordered by phone (800-323-7619) and picked up at the cruise boat office near the city dock or can be purchased directly at the office. Seating is on a "first come-first served basis. Since seating on the upper deck is limited it is recommended that passengers arrive at the boat's loading area as soon as they can. You should attempt to be at the boat loading location at least a half hour before departure. Although the schedule of service varies from year to year the normal cruise schedule has the following trips:

A daily Grand Tour from mid-May to mid-October, lasting 3-¼ hours, that leaves at 10:00 AM. This narrated cruise makes no stops in the islands but goes out to the north shore of Devils Island, weather permitting, for a viewing of the spectacular sea caves there. This shore of Devils Island is Wisconsin's most northern point.

A Raspberry Island cruise from July 1st to Labor Day, lasting four hours, that leaves at 1:30 PM on Tuesdays and weekends. See the chapter titled Raspberry Island for your options once on the island. Check with cruise service time for possible schedule changes from year to year.

A Stockton Island cruise from July 1st to Labor Day, lasting 4-½ hours, that leaves at 8:30 AM, on

Tuesdays and weekends. See the chapter titled Stockton Island for your options once on the island. Check with cruise service for possible schedule changes from year to year.

Contact the cruise boat office for other cruise trips that may be available during the time of your visit. If your visit to the area will take place during the Lighthouse Celebration in early September there are options available for visits to Devils, Sand and Michigan Islands.

The Madeline Island Ferry dock is located north of the main city dock, and has ferries running to Madeline Island approximately every half hour during the summer. The trip takes approximately twenty minutes. Obtain a schedule at the ferry office adjacent to the ferry loading area. For those taking the ferry a map of Madeline Island is available. See the chapter titled Madeline Island for options once on the island.

Water taxi service to any of the islands is provided by several operators. See the reference section at the end of the book for a listing of these operators. There is normally a flat fee for a round trip, which covers both drop off and pickup—although drop off and pickup may be separated by a number of hours or days. The flat charge varies depending on the distance of the island from Bayfield. The cost per passenger obviously decreases as the number of passengers transported on the trip increases. The maximum carried varies by operator.

BY SAILBOAT

There are two sailboat options available to the visitor who wants to see and/or visit the islands—captained or bareboat charters. A list of the captained charters available can be found in the reference section. Some can be as short as a half-day or can extend over several days. Some may include other passengers. Although most leave from the Bayfield City Dock, others depart from other marinas in the area.

Bareboat charters require that the individual leasing the sailboat have sufficient experience in sailing. This is usually presented to the chartering office in the form of a resume. An "on water" test by the charterer may be required. Normally, bareboat charters are made well in advance, however check with the charterer on boat availability at the time of your visit.

There are two major bareboat charterers in the Bayfield area—Sailboats, Inc. (800-826-7010) and Superior Charters, Inc. (800-772-5124). For those willing to invest the time to learn how to sail, either of these charterers conducts training classes. A list of other sailing schools can be found in the reference section. Bareboat charters can also be arranged on Madeline Island through the Madeline Island Yacht Club (800-821-3480).

Bareboat chartering allows the captain and his crew to set their own sailing itinerary and visit any of the Apostle Islands—one of the most outstanding experiences that sailing has to offer. Most sailboats have dinghies, capable of carrying up to three people, available for reaching the island shores or entering into the sea caves on quiet days.

It is strongly recommended that anyone obtaining a bareboat charter review information regarding boating in the Apostle Islands before proceeding—as a minimum the Apostle Islands NOAA chart (#14973) and a book describing some of the nautical and weather hazards in the islands. Books of this type can be found in the reference section under "Apostle Islands".

BY POWERBOAT

For those visitors bringing their own powerboats to the Apostle Islands area, there are convenient launching sites available. These are listed at the end of this section. As with bareboat sailboat chartering it is recommended that the power boater obtain some information regarding boating in the Apostle Islands before proceeding—as a minimum the Apostle Islands chart (#14973) and a book describing some of the nautical and weather hazards in the islands. Books of this type can be found in the reference section under "Apostle Islands".

Although the National Park Service (NPS) does not recommend the use of open boats less than 16 feet in length for travel among the islands, the current and forecasted weather should be the deciding factor. At times smaller boats are perfectly safe, and at other times even large boats should stay off the water. Obviously, the use of one's common-sense is paramount to any hard and fast rules. The NPS also warns against overloading the rated capacity of the boat. The following excerpt is taken from a NPS brochure: "Boaters must obey U. S. Coast Guard inland navigation rules. Each boat must have: an appropriate personal flotation device (PFD) for each person on board, fire extinguisher, whistle or horn, marker lights, and a manual bailing device. All children under age 13 aboard boats underway must wear an appropriate PFD except when they are below decks or in an enclosed cabin."

In addition, depending on the boat's size, the following equipment should be carried: a compass, appropriate anchor, lines, marine band radio, cell phone, Geographic Position System (GPS) receiver, radar reflector, first aid kit, tools, spare parts and signal flares.

Other than Madeline Island, there are no facilities for refueling in the Apostle Islands, so plan accordingly. A common rule of thumb is a $1/3^{rd}$ of gas consumption going to your destination, a $1/3^{rd}$ coming back, and a $1/3^{rd}$ as a safety factor. Keep a constant eye on your fuel level.

Boat launching ramps can be found in Ashland, Washburn, Bayfield, Red Cliff, Cornucopia and La Pointe. Inquire at the local marinas for exact launch locations. Some require launching fees. There is also a launching ramp near the Sand Bay Visitor's Center at the east end of the mainland portion of the National Lakeshore, north of Red Cliff, and another, about two miles east of Ashland, off Highway 2, at the end of Reykdal Road. The Reykdal Road landing is the best launching point for those wishing cruise Chequamegon Bay and visit the Kakagon Sloughs. No launch fee is required at this location.

BY KAYAK

There are five kayak suppliers in the Apostle Islands area, four on the mainland and one on Madeline Island. See the listings in the reference section. Among the services provided by these suppliers are those involving guided trips of several kayaks. For those bringing their own kayaks to the area they can be launched from mainland locations at Bayfield (beach north of ferry landing), Little Sand Bay and Meyers Beach, at the west end of the mainland portion of the National Lakeshore. A visit to the Apostle Islands National Lakeshore Headquarters in Bayfield is recommended prior to embarking on your trip. Request the brochure "Paddling In The Apostles". The cruise boat will transport kayaks on their normal visits to the islands for a fee.

CHARTER FISHING

There are several charter fishing services in the Apostle Islands area. See the reference section. Accommodations for half or full day trips are usually available, but advance reservations are preferred.

FLOAT PLANS

If you travel among the islands in your own boat it's wise to have a float plan prepared before you leave and give it to a friend or leave it with a responsible person in the marina. It should indicate your route and expected time of return.

BAYFIELD—
GATEWAY TO THE APOSTLES

It's difficult to discuss the Apostle Islands without also commenting at length about the town of Bayfield, from which most all visits to the islands begin.

Located on State Highway 13, which circles around the Bayfield peninsula, in Wisconsin's northern reaches, Bayfield, founded in 1856, with a current population of approximately 600, strikes one as a New England fishing village in many aspects. The town fathers have, to their credit, not allowed any of the franchise businesses one would normally encounter in other towns and cities. Instead there is a main street (Rittenhouse Avenue) which contains various retail stores and restaurants, having, in most cases, a distinctive retro flavor of a time when life was unhurried and more relaxed—although during the busy holiday periods that feeling can get a little frayed as it becomes crowded. If possible, visit Bayfield outside the holiday periods to appreciate the charm of this town. There are also many bed and breakfast operations in the area. Bayfield was cited as the "Best Little Town in the Midwest" based on an extensive survey conducted by the Chicago Tribune.

It is here that you will find most of the service businesses that offer visitors the ability to visit the islands. The Apostle Islands Cruise Service offices are located at the foot of Rittenhouse Avenue on the lakefront. The ferry service to Madeline Island is located approximately one block north of Rittenhouse Avenue on the lakeshore. Most of the captained sailboat tours leave from the city dock. Information regarding all of these offerings is contained in the reference section at the rear of this book.

THE APOSTLE ISLANDS NATIONAL LAKESHORE HEADQUARTERS

Located just one block north of Rittenhouse Avenue, on Washington Street, between North 5th St. and North 4th St., the Apostle Islands National Lakeshore Headquarters should be the starting point for those wishing to get an initial understanding of the islands. Visitors are encouraged to view the 20-minute film that is available for viewing by request. Spend a little time at the center reviewing the exhibits, including a 3rd order Fresnel lens, which was the primary means of focusing the light that went out from the lighthouses in the islands in years past. This particular lens was originally installed in the Michigan Island lighthouse. Staff personnel at the center are very helpful and will answer your questions. A diverse selection of free brochures are available, including those describing the more-visited islands, camping, boating, kayaking, camping and scuba diving. In addition a wide variety of books on subjects pertinent to the islands are available for purchase. An interesting bit of history regarding the building housing the headquarters is that it served as a German POW facility during 1944-45.

POINTS OF INTEREST

In addition to the interesting and varied retail shops on Rittenhouse Avenue, the following places should be visited, time permitting.

The Chamber of Commerce office, located one block south of Rittenhouse Avenue, on the northeast corner of Manypenny Avenue and Broad St., has many free brochures describing activities in the area—and the personnel are very helpful. Be sure to pick up the free booklet published by Bayfield that contains a map of Bayfield plus information on businesses in the area.

Greunke's Restaurant and First Street Inn located on the northwest corner of Rittenhouse Avenue and North 1st St., has a 40's/50's décor. It was here that John Kennedy, Jr. and his friends spent a night and had breakfast in August 1995, before kayaking in the islands. The restaurant is known for the regional delicacy of whitefish livers.

The Old Rittenhouse Inn, located at the western end of Rittenhouse Avenue, on the northwest corner of the intersection with North 3rd St. is one of the most famous "bed and breakfast" inns in Wisconsin—if not the country. Managed by Mary and Jerry Phillips for many years, it is now under the capable direction of their daughter, Wendy, The inn's Landmark Restaurant serves gourmet meals in a Victorian setting. During the summer, outstanding floral arrangements decorate the porch.

The Keeper of the Light retail store, adjacent to the cruise service ticketing office, has an interesting and extensive collection of nautical merchandise and is the coordinating office for the Lighthouse Celebration cruises held in early September.

The Manypenny Bistro, a breakfast spot, located on Manypenny Avenue, one block south of Rittenhouse Avenue, at the northwest corner of the intersection with South 2nd St. is frequented by many sailors, before they depart on their boats into the islands.

Maggie's, a red-hued building, located at the western end of Manypenny Avenue, is open for lunch and dinner. Don't expect a far north décor of moose heads and deer antlers—it's strictly a Caribbean decorative flavor here—with lots of pink flamingos— and the food is delicious.

If you're looking for a quiet change of pace, stop in the What Goes 'Round bookstore located just off the northeast corner of the intersection of Manypenny Avenue and South Second St. Many book treasures can be found here. Another fine bookstore is located on the 100 block of Rittenhouse Avenue—Apostle Islands Booksellers.

There are two museums in the area. The Bayfield Maritime Museum located on the lake front, south of Rittenhouse Avenue, on the northwest corner of Wilson Avenue and South 1st. St., will give you an appreciation for the history of the area and for those who braved the cold waters of Lake Superior. Dave Strzok, the former owner of the cruise service, was the driving force behind the establishment of this museum. There is also a museum describing the history of Bayfield located just off the southeast corner of Washington Avenue and North Broad Street that has several interesting exhibits.

The lakefront area, two blocks south of Rittenhouse Avenue, is the place to obtain freshly caught whitefish or lake trout fillets for dinner. Two fish purveyors are located here.

An extensive area of apple orchards is located west of Bayfield, in the high hills above the town. A map of the orchards can be obtained, free of charge, at the Chamber of Commerce office in Bayfield. In addition to the apple crop available in the fall, many of the orchards have fields of strawberries, raspberries and blueberries, some available for public picking throughout the summer months. If visiting during late May or early June be sure to view the orchards when the apple trees are in bloom. Blue Vista Farm and Erickson Orchard are recommended.

The Eckels Pottery Gallery is about a mile south of Bayfield on Highway 13. If you're lucky you'll see pottery being made here, as the workshop is adjacent to the showroom.

Just a short distance further south on Highway 13 you can pick up a fresh pie or other freshly baked goods at Gourmet Garage, a working kitchen and store. You can't miss the large "Pies" sign by the side of the road.

For those interested in spectacular views of the islands while golfing there is the Apostle Highlands Golf Course, south of Bayfield. The view from the 3rd tee and fairway overlooking Madeline Island and Long Island with the surrounding waters is breathtaking. They can be contacted at 877-222-4053.

The Bayfield Fish Hatchery is located about three miles south of Bayfield on Highway 13 and is open to the public.

Big Top Chautauqua is located about three miles south of Bayfield, off Highway 13. Various musical attractions are presented during summer evenings under a big-top circus tent. Among the talented performers who have performed here are Johnny Cash and Willie Nelson. If possible, try to see the performance of "Riding The Wind", an excellent musical exposition of Bayfield and the Apostle Islands. A list of the current attractions can be found in the Chamber of Commerce office in Bayfield. They can be contacted at 888-244-8368.

Also south of Bayfield on Highway 13 are the Pike's Bay and Port Superior Marianas. The Portside Restaurant, located on the second floor of a building in the Port Superior Marina, has excellent food and an outstanding view of the harbor.

If your visit to the area occurs from mid to late June you can see the lupines in bloom. They are found growing profusely between Bayfield and Washburn along Highway 13 and along the orchard roads west of Bayfield.

There are many other fine restaurants and lodging establishments in the area. Again, the brochures found in the Chamber of Commerce building will give you further information.

And one final note—the most important event on the Bayfield calendar, the Apple Festival, "Applefest", is held on the first weekend in October. This is the highlight of the fall season and the streets of the town are crowded. In addition to several booths of apple related goods there are many others selling everything from soup to nuts—literally. Parking space is at a premium so be prepared for a long walk.

BAYFIELD

Bayfield, looking southwest

Cruise boat and ferry loading areas

BAYFIELD

Apostle Islands National Lakeshore Headquarters

View from 3rd tee of Apostle Highlands Golf Course

Lupines in bloom in mid-June

Apostle Islands Marina on the Bayfield waterfront

MADELINE ISLAND

Madeline Island is the largest of the Apostle Islands, and the easiest to visit. The island was not included in the Apostle Islands National Lakeshore when it was formed in 1970 because of the extent of private ownership on the island. A ferry runs between the city dock at Bayfield and the dock at La Pointe on Madeline Island every half hour during the summer days. A ferry schedule and a map of the island can be obtained from the ferry office. Vehicles can also be transported on the ferry. The office can be reached at 715-747-2051.

The island has 45 miles of paved roads, which allows the visitor to travel throughout the island. Madeline's year-round community of about 200 swells to 2500 during the summer. The island has a rich and varied history, beginning with early Indian activity and continuing into the 17th century as an important outpost of French exploration and fur trading. A visitor to the island can obtain an understanding of this history by visiting the Madeline Island Museum just east of the dock. Previously bearing the Indian name for the golden-breasted woodpecker, the island received its modern name from the daughter of the Indian chief White Crane, when she converted to Christianity.

LA POINTE
Located at the island's northwest corner, La Pointe is the oldest European settlement in Wisconsin, although its original location was at the west end of Long Island, before moving to Madeline Island. The town has a main street containing several commercial establishments, including the Beach Club, which has

the best whitefish sandwich in the Apostle Islands area and Tom's Burned Down Cafe, which should be visited to experience its uniqueness. Rental mopeds and bicycles are available at the south end of La Pointe's main street. (715-747-6585).

OTHER POINTS OF INTEREST

Just south of La Pointe is the Madeline Island Yacht Club Marina and the Madeline Island golf course, with as one might expect, spectacular views.

There is an island-studded lagoon, best seen from atop a bluff near the Big Bay Town Park picnic area at the north end of Big Bay, considered by many to be the most scenic spot in the islands. Day use of this park and beach is free. Rental canoes and rowboats are available for use in the lagoon (715-747-2685). Fishing is allowed (Wisconsin license required).

Big Bay State Park, which occupies a significant part of the middle of the island, has an extensive trail system, 55 camping sites and scenic picnic areas. A brochure, available at the park entrance, contains a map of the park. An entrance fee is required.

MADELINE ISLAND

Madeline Island looking southwest

La Pointe

MADELINE ISLAND

View of lagoon from Big Bay Town Park

Bridge over lagoon

MADELINE ISLAND

Lagoon inlet from Lake Superior

Kayak entering lagoon inlet

MADELINE ISLAND

View from picnic area in Big Bay State Park

Exotic animals at private farm on Big Bay Road

STOCKTON ISLAND

Stockton Island is the second largest island of the Apostles and is the most visited island in the National Lakeshore. Signs of human activity along Quarry and Presque Isle Bays date back hundreds of years.

OPTIONS UPON LANDING
After the cruise boat lands at the island's dock there is sufficient time to explore a portion of the island by taking any of the following hikes:

- A short ½ mile hike to Julian Bay beach passes by one of the most scenic attractions in the islands—the Tombolo Bog Overlook. This hike is normally led by a Park Service employee, who meets passengers debarking from the cruise boat on the dock.

- For those wishing a more physical experience, a hike along the Anderson Point Trail, which circles Presque Isle Point, is recommended. The start of this 1-½ mile trail is just a short distance up the Julian Bay trail. This hike follows the shore of Presque Isle Point and allows the hiker to experience the spectacular views along the rugged coastline. Hikers should be careful to avoid tripping hazards on the trail in the form of embedded roots and rocks. The trail ends at Julian Bay beach and hooks up with the trail coming from the bog overlook that leads back to the dock. Many downed trees are evident during this hike, bearing testament to the severity of storms in the area and the sandy topsoil in which the trees are weakly rooted.

- For those hikers wishing a longer hike, follow the three-mile Tombolo Trail along the Julian Bay beach, which circles back along the bog and the Presque Isle Bay camping sites to the dock. Be aware that occasionally the inlet to the bog from the lake is open about ¾ mile up the beach and could be knee deep. If taking this trail from mid-July to mid-August you may find blueberries along the trail through the woods, if the black bears haven't gotten to them first.

Please note that time constraints for return to the cruise boat would not normally allow a hiker to do both the Anderson Point Trail and the Tombolo Trail on the same day—unless you're a fast hiker and don't stop to appreciate the spectacular views.

SPECIAL NOTE ON BEARS
Stockton Island is known for its large black bear population. Although it is unlikely you will encounter a bear you should keep in mind the following cautionary words included in publications of the National Park Service. "Never approach or feed a bear. Keep a distance of at least 50 yards, even for photography. If you encounter a bear in a visitor use area, make yourself look big, yell, make noise until the bear leaves the area, and report the encounter to park staff as soon as possible."

Please understand that if you make a bear feel comfortable in the presence of people you may be signing the bear's death warrant since bears that lose their fear of people and frequent camping areas have to be destroyed. Obviously, being in close proximity to a mother bear with a cub is a situation to be avoided. If you see a lone cub leave the area quickly, but do not run.

CAMPING
Stockton Island has the best camping facilities in the Apostles. The camping sites are situated on a bluff overlooking Presque Isle Bay. Camping permits are required and should be purchased, in advance, at the Apostle Islands National Lakeshore Headquarters in Bayfield. Each camping site has a picnic table, a tent pad, a fire pit and a bear-proof locker to store food. Most evenings, weather permitting, the local Park Service employee on the island conducts informative sessions regarding the islands, around a campfire circle, just south of the visitor center.

Stockton Island looking northeast

STOCKTON ISLAND

Bog Overlook

Julian Bay Beach and Presque Isle Point

RASPBERRY ISLAND

Raspberry Island is known for two outstanding features—a beautiful lighthouse complex and a scenic bay used for overnight anchorages by many boaters.

OPTIONS UPON LANDING
- Most visitors coming to Raspberry Island for the first time take the lighthouse grounds tour, which requires a small fee. This tour is conducted by a Park Service interpreter. An optional climb up to the lighthouse deck via of a winding staircase is a part of this tour. There is a beautiful flower garden maintained on the lighthouse grounds, the origin of which dates back to the 1920's. The original lighthouse was built in 1863, about the time the Gettysburg battle of the Civil War was being fought. That lighthouse no longer stands although the original foundation anchors the current property. Raspberry Island was one of the few Apostle Islands to escape the woodman's axe due to a federal policy that reserved a substantial portion of the area around a lighthouse for the keeper's use.

- You can take a hike to the East Bay Beach, about a ½ mile from the lighthouse grounds. East Bay is a sheltered bay, north of a sandspit, that is a prized anchorage for sailboats. The beach is beautiful and after a period of hot weather, swimmers and waders can be seen here. An interesting attraction on the beach is an uprooted tree that contains "wishing" rocks put in the dead tree's gnarled roots.

- You can also take a hike to the Raspberry Island Overlook on the west side of the island. This 1-¼ mile trail leads to a high cliff overlooking the lake, from which the Sand Island lighthouse can be seen in the distance—a duty that was once required of the Raspberry Island lighthouse keepers. This trail is not maintained and requires climbing over and ducking under fallen trees.

Raspberry Island looking north

RASPBERRY ISLAND

Raspberry Island Lighthouse

Aerial view of lighthouse grounds

RASPBERRY ISLAND

Raspberry Island Overlook

Wishing Rock Tree on East Bay Beach

LONG ISLAND AND CHEQUAMEGON BAY

Long Island, unlike the other Apostle Islands, is a barrier spit, composed entirely of sand. It hasn't really been an island since the summer of 1976, as wave and wind actions closed the gap between the island's eastern end and the western end of the mainland (Chequamegon Point). The island is frequently visited by powerboaters since it is in close proximity to the marinas along Chequamegon Bay.

The island has a lighthouse (La Pointe) midway on its north side and a large navigation light tower at its western end, marking the entrance to Chequamegon Bay, where the cities of Ashland and Washburn are located. The light tower stands next to an abandoned light station, recently renovated, that was originally constructed in 1896.

Care should be taken when walking along the beach on the island's lakeside in late spring or early summer as it represents one of the few nesting spots for the piping plover, an endangered shore bird. The young chicks have been compared to yellow fluff balls on toothpicks as they run along the beach. Do not allow dogs to run free on the beach. Dogs are required to be on leashes throughout the National Lakeshore.

This island also is known for having substantial patches of poison ivy so be aware of its characteristics and keep a sharp eye. Deer, bears and foxes have been sighted on Long Island.

There is a trail from the La Pointe Lighthouse to the Chequamegon Point light tower at the island's western tip.

There is a long deep beach on the north side of the Island that extends along the mainland peninsula all the way to the mouth of Bad River, a total distance of about ten miles. The mainland area is part of the Bad River Indian Reservation. The Chequamegon Bay side of the island also has substantial beach areas.

One of the most beautiful and serene ecosystems in the area can be found at the northeast end of Chequamegon Bay on the Bad River Indian Reservation—the Kakagon Sloughs. This is an area of waterways that meander through "seas of grass". Wild rice grows here and water lilies are abundant.

Long Island showing attachment to mainland

OTHER ISLANDS

BASSWOOD
This island is one of the closest of the Apostles to the mainland, being separated by only about a mile of water, near Red Cliff. It has a dock about half way up its west side and has a trail that circles the island. Some abandoned sandstone quarries are located at its southeast corner. An island landmark, Honeymoon Rock, is located off its north shore.

Basswood Island looking north

BASSWOOD ISLAND

Honeymoon Rock

Basswood Island Dock

BEAR

Bear Island and Oak Island were the only Apostle Islands above water about 5000 years ago before the waters level fell to about 600 feet above sea level. There are no public trails or docks on the island. A large sandspit is found at its southern end.

Bear Island looking northwest

BEAR ISLAND

Sandspit

Northeast Beach

CAT
This island, shaped somewhat like a cat with a stunted head, has extensive beaches on its east and west shores, in the vicinity of the cat's "neck". There are no trails or docks on the island.

Cat Island looking south

CAT ISLAND

Sandspit

East Beach

CAT ISLAND

North end of island

Sea Arch at island's north end

DEVILS

This island, known for its beautifully formed sea caves at its northern end, is difficult to approach or land upon unless wave conditions permit, since it has no beaches. There is a lighthouse complex at the island's north end and a small rock-strewn harbor at its south end, connected by a trail, which was once a road that runs up the center of the island.

Devils Island looking south

DEVILS ISLAND

Sea Caves

Sea Caves

DEVILS ISLAND

Devils Island Lighthouse

DEVILS ISLAND

West side shore

Inside Sea Cave

DEVILS ISLAND

Another view of Devils Island Lighthouse

Dock area at south end of island

DEVILS ISLAND

Sea Cave Columns

Sea Cave Columns

EAGLE

This small 28-acre island, located at the western end of the Apostle Islands, has been designated as a bird sanctuary from May 15 to September 1, and is off limits to visitors during that period. There are no trails on the island and it is difficult to land on.

Eagle Island looking south

GULL

Smallest of the Apostle Islands at three acres, Gull Island is just northeast of Michigan Island. No visitation is allowed on this island during May 15 to September 1, since it is a bird sanctuary.

Guano covered Gull Island looking northwest

HERMIT

Situated between Basswood and Stockton Islands in the North Channel, this island once had active sandstone quarries and apple orchards. Its original name was Wilson's Island, after the hermit who lived there. There are no docks or trails on the island. An island landmark, Lookout Point, is located off its northeast shore.

Hermit Island looking northwest

Lookout Point

IRONWOOD
Known for its sandspit at its southern end, this island has no docks or trails.

Ironwood Island looking west

Sandspit

MANITOU

Located northwest of Stockton Island this island is known for two important features—a dangerous rock strewn and shallow area leading out to Little Manitou, a pile of rocks with a flashing light off Manitou's southwest corner, and a deserted fish camp at its southern end, which has been maintained by the Park Service.

Manitou Island looking north

Historic Fish Camp

MANITOU ISLAND

Little Manitou with cormorants

View showing Little Manitou and Fish Camp

MICHIGAN

Located southeast of Stockton Island and northeast of Madeline Island, Michigan Island is known for the beautiful sandspit at its southwest end and the two lighthouses on its southern shore in the vicinity of a dock not far from the sandspit. There is a trail from the sandspit to the lighthouses and a side trail that leads to a lagoon, a short distance from the sandspit.

Michigan Island looking southwest

MICHIGAN ISLAND

Lighthouses and dock

Sandspit

NORTH TWIN
Formerly known as Brownstone Island, this island's most striking feature is the brownstone slabs surrounding much of the island. There are no docks or trails on the island. The island is one of the few in the Apostle Islands archipelago not stripped of its lumber due to its remoteness and lack of easy access.

North Twin Island looking south

NORTH TWIN ISLAND

North Twin Island looking southwest

North Twin Island looking north

OAK

Oak Island is the tallest island in the Apostles and has deep ravines and steep hills. It has an extensive trail system, one of which leads out to a high overlook on the north end of the island. There is a dock midway up its west shore.

Oak Island looking east

Oak Island cliff and overlook

OAK ISLAND

Sandspit

View from Oak Island Overlook

OTTER

Otter Island has a dock at its southern end and a trail that leads to its northern shore. This heavily forested island is best known for the 1960 Boy Scouts Camporee of almost 1500 scouts that was held on it. There is a bird refuge area on the northwest shore, which prohibits visitation to that part of the island between May 15 and September 1.

Otter Island looking southeast

Otter Island looking north

OUTER

Third largest of the Apostle Islands, and standing like a sentinel at the far northeast corner of the Apostles, Outer is known for its extensive sandspit at its southern end and the lighthouse at its northern end. A 7-½ mile trail leads from the sandspit to the lighthouse. The dock in the vicinity of the lighthouse is only usable by shallow draft boats when wave conditions are low, due to the rocks and boulders in the area.

Outer Island looking north

Sandspit

OUTER ISLAND

Outer Island dock and lighthouse

Outer Island lagoon

OUTER ISLAND

Northeast shore

Outer Island Lighthouse

ROCKY

This strangely shaped island, located in the upper reaches of the Apostles, along with South Twin Island, forms a sheltered area from most winds. The island has extensive beach areas, some of which are still under private leases. There is a dock at the island's southeast corner and trails leading from it to a sandspit and an overlook.

Rocky Island looking south

SAND

Located at the western end of the Apostles, north of Little Sand Bay and the Town of Russell on the mainland, this island once had a town named Shaw, which was active in the late nineteenth and early twentieth century. It has a lighthouse at its northern end that is considered by many to be the most beautiful in the islands. It has a dock midway up its eastern shore in East Bay, and trails, one leading to the lighthouse and another leading to the south end of the island. The West Bay area facing the mainland still has some private life leases.

Sand Island looking southwest

Sand Island's north shore

SAND ISLAND

Swallow Point Sea Caves

Justice Bay and Swallow Point (left side of bay)

SAND ISLAND

Justice Bay

Sand Island Lighthouse

SOUTH TWIN

Located just east of Rocky Island forming the area that protects boaters from most winds encountered, this island once had an airfield. A trail leads from the dock to the overgrown airfield.

South Twin looking southwest

Sailboats at anchor off South Twin—Rocky Island in background.

YORK

Located between Sand and Raspberry Islands, York is strangely shaped, looking somewhat like a club with a crooked handle. There is an extensive beach on its north shore and a sandspit on its southeast corner. There are no docks are trails on the island.

York Island looking east

YORK ISLAND

North Beach

Sandspit

RECOMMENDED ACTIVITIES

- Take Grand Tour cruise on excursion boat.

- Take ferry to Madeline Island

- Explore Madeline Island by car, moped, bicycle or tour bus.

- Take excursion boat tours to Stockton and Raspberry Islands.

- Hike around Presque Isle Point on Stockton Island (Anderson Point Trail).

- Hike along Julian Bay Beach and Tombolo Trail on Stockton Island.

- Take tour of lighthouse grounds on Raspberry Island and go up into lighthouse.

- Hike from the lighthouse complex on Raspberry Island to the East Beach sandspit.

- Walk along Big Bay beach on Madeline Island.

- Take excursion cruise boat to Sand and Michigan islands during September's Lighthouse Celebration.

- Take captained sailboat cruise of islands.

- Drive to Little Sand Bay section of Apostle Island National Lakeshore on mainland, north of Red Cliff, and hike along lake shore.

- Camp overnight on Stockton Island along Presque Isle Bay.

- Take charter fishing cruise.

- Visit Apostle Islands National Lakeshore Headquarters in Bayfield.

- Visit Northern Great Lakes Visitor Center, west of Ashland.

- Visit Madeline Island Museum.

- Visit Bayfield Maritime Museum

LIGHTHOUSES

Ashland Chequamegon Bay Breakwater

Long Island—La Pointe

LIGHTHOUSES

Long Island—Chequamegon Point

Michigan Island (1857)

LIGHTHOUSES

Michigan Island (1929)

LIGHTHOUSES

Michigan Island- both lighthouses

Raspberry Island

LIGHTHOUSES

Outer Island

LIGHTHOUSES

Sand Island

LIGHTHOUSES

Devils Island

MAJOR BEACHES

Big Bay Beach—Madeline Island

Julian Bay Beach—Stockton Island

North Shore Beach—Long Island

MAJOR BEACHES

East Bay Beach—Raspberry Island

Sandspit—Michigan Island

Sandspit—Outer Island

MAJOR BEACHES

Justice Bay Beach—Sand Island

Lighthouse Bay Beach—Sand Island

East Bay Beach—Sand Island

BEACH STONES

BEACH STONES

SURROUNDING COMMUNITIES

ASHLAND

Situated on the southern shore of Chequamegon Bay, Ashland is the largest community in the Apostle Islands region—population approximately 8,200. It was the hub of the region's industrial activity that began in the mid-nineteenth century and continued into the 20th. At one time it had five ore docks loading huge ships, some more than two football fields in length that carried iron ore to the industrial Midwest steel mills. The last ore shipment left Ashland in 1965. Only one ore dock remained in 2012 and its owner, Canadian National Railway, began demolition in that year, completing the razing in 2013.

Ashland is the major retailing center in the area, having a Super Wal-Mart (located off Highway 2 on Ashland's eastern edge), an indoor water park in the AmericInn, other large consumer outlets and several fast food franchises. The office of the area's major newspaper, The Daily Press, can also be found here. Ashland's downtown area has been revitalized with many new boutique shops and an excellent restaurant and brewery—Deep Water Grille. However, there are still some structures in the area that evoke memories of the past, including the Bay Theatre (built in 1937), the Vaughn library, (established in 1886), the Huhn's drug store located in a former Masonic Lodge facility, a huge County Building with cavernous halls, a City Hall located in a brownstone building and the refurbished Soo Line Depot, another outstanding example of brownstone construction. Many of the city's building walls contain beautiful murals depicting its past. Ashland was named Historic Mural Capital of Wisconsin. Stop in at the city's Chamber of Commerce to obtain a map showing the location of all the murals.

The majestic Hotel Chequamegon, located on the lakefront, next to the city's band shell, was constructed in a style reminiscent of a former hotel of the same name that stood across the street back in the late nineteenth century. The lobby and sitting room have a distinctive late nineteenth century ambience. The hotel has a restaurant and bar located downstairs, Molly Cooper's, which has a large outdoor porch overlooking the marina and Chequamegon Bay where, when weather permits, meals and drinks are served. From this vantage point a diner has one of the best views available of the sun setting over the Bayfield hills. Be sure to read the history of the bar's name.

On the city's western edge you will find an excellent Mexican restaurant, El Dorado, and the Platter Restaurant located in an historic brownstone building, which once was a house of ill repute for the upper class of the area in the late nineteenth century. Presidential candidate John F. Kennedy had dinner here during one of his trips to the area during the Wisconsin primary season of 1960.

On the southern edge of Ashland is the Northland College campus, consisting of several buildings spread over a large area. The college is a well-respected center of learning dealing with environmental issues.

West of Ashland, off Highway 2, just beyond the intersection of Highways 2 and 13, is the Northern Great Lakes Visitor Center. This large facility has many interesting exhibits relevant to the area.

East of Ashland, at the northeast end of Chequamegon Bay, can be found the Kakagon Sloughs, a part of the Bad River Indian Reservation. This is an area of quiet waterways that can best be described as uniquely serene. Also located on the reservation, approximately eight miles east of Ashland on Highway 2, in Odanah, is the Bad River Casino and Resort.

Ashland looking south from Chequamegon Bay

Entrance to Kakagon Sloughs

Ashland's last ore dock

CORNUCOPIA

Home of Wisconsin's northernmost post office, this small fishing community has a marina, a beautiful beach in Siskiwit Bay, a general store and a large community building, which is the site of the region's best fish fry, an all-you-can-eat affair, held on the first Sunday in July. Many of the town's citizens participate in this annual event, including youngsters who circulate among the long community style tables with plates of extra fish. It's a simple set fare meal of deep fried whitefish, homemade potato salad, bread, butter, green onions and radishes. Coffee and lemonade are also served. Get there early if you want to avoid the long lines that start forming at 10:00 AM. Another well-attended town event is Corny Day, held on the second Saturday in August. Be sure to stop by the Green Shed Museum near the harbor.

Cornucopia,
on Siskiwit Bay of Lake Superior

RED CLIFF

Home of the Red Cliff Band of Lake Superior Chippewa, Red Cliff has a small harbor located along the West Channel across from Basswood Island. The Legendary Waters Resort and Casino was completed in 2011. Red Cliff is the site of the colorful Tribal Pow-Wow held on the July 4th weekend. For more information go to www.redcliff.org. One of the major kayak suppliers on the mainland, Living Adventures, Inc., is located here—on the east side of Highway 13, on the southern edge of Red Cliff. Just north of Red Cliff is the Little Sand Bay section of the Apostle Islands National Lakeshore. Take County Highway K, off Highway 13.

Red Cliff,
on Buffalo Bay of Lake Superior

WASHBURN

Located on the western shore of Chequamegon Bay, Washburn has a marina, a museum and bookstore, both housed in old brownstone buildings across from each other, the Stage North theatre which presents a variety of live entertainment, an IGA supermarket and several restaurants. There is a long established crafts shop selling paintings, sculptures and art related supplies, Karlyn's Gallery, located on Washburn's main street (Highway 13). The talented owner, Karlyn Holman, conducts art classes that are well attended. About 1-½ miles north of Washburn is Houghton Falls Road that leads to a newly opened trail that follows a scenic forested canyon to the water's edge. The public parking area is located approximately a ¼ mile before the road ends.

Washburn,
on the northern shore of Chequamegon Bay

SOURCES FOR ADDITIONAL INFORMATION

Apostle Islands

Holzhueter, John O., *Madeline Island and the Chequamegon Region,* Madison: The State Historical Society of Wisconsin, 1986. A historical review of Madeline Island and the surrounding region.

National Park Service, *A Guide to Apostle Islands National Lakeshore,* Washington: Department of Publications, U. S. Department of the Interior, 1988. Official National Park Handbook for the Apostle Islands National Lakeshore.

National Park Service, DVD/VHS, *On the Edge of Gichigami—Voices of the Apostle Islands,* Produced by Harper's Ferry Center (20 min).

Newman, Lawrence, *The Apostle Islands—America's Wilderness in the Water,* South Elgin: Silver Millennium Publications, Inc., 2008. A guide for boaters, kayakers, campers and beachcombers.

Newman, Lawrence, *Sailing Adventures In The Apostle Islands,* South Elgin: Silver Millennium Publications, Inc., 2011. The cruising guide for boaters in the Apostle Islands.

Rennicke, Jeff, photographs by Layne Kennedy, *Jewels on the Water,* Friends of the Apostle Islands National Lakeshore, 2005. Photographic review of Apostle Islands history—both past and present.

Ross, Hamilton, *La Pointe: Village Outpost on Madeline Island,* Madison: State Historical Society, 2000. History of La Pointe and Madeline Island.

Strzok, Dave, *A Visitor's Guide to the Apostle Islands National Lakeshore,* Ashland: Superior Printing and Specialties, 1999. A comprehensive review of the islands and their history, including useful information for those boating, hiking and camping in the islands.

Official website for the Apostle Islands National Lakeshore: nps.gov/apis

The Apostle Islands National Lakeshore Headquarters in Bayfield has an assortment of free brochures describing the more visited islands and several providing useful information on hiking, camping, boating, scuba diving and kayaking activities in the islands.

Area Information
Ashland Area Chamber of Commerce
1716 Lake Shore Drive West
Ashland, WI 54806
800-284-9484/715-682-2500
travelashlandcounty.com

Bayfield County Tourism
117 E. 6th Street
Washburn, WI 54891
800-472-6338
travelbayfieldcounty.com

Bayfield Chamber of Commerce and Visitors Bureau
42 S. Broad St.
Bayfield, WI 54814
800-447-4094/715-779-3335
bayfield.org

Madeline Island Chamber of Commerce
PO Box 274
La Pointe, WI 54850
888-475-3386/715-747-2801
madelineisland.com

Washburn Area Chamber of Commerce
126 W. Bayfield St.
Washburn, WI 54891
800-253-4495/715-373-5017

Big Top Chautauqua
3 miles south of Bayfield, west of Highway 13
715-373-5552/888-244-8368
www.bigtop.org

Boating Regulations
Wisconsin Boating Regulations—obtain at marinas and the Apostle Islands National Lakeshore Headquarters in Bayfield. Can also be obtained directly from the Wisconsin Department of Natural Resources, PO Box 7921, Madison, WI 53707

Camping—National Lakeshore
National Park Service
Apostle Islands National Lakeshore Headquarters
415 Washington Ave
Bayfield, WI 54814
715-779-3397
Camping permits can be obtained in Bayfield or at the National Park Service office in Little Sand Bay. Request the brochure "Camping in the Apostle Islands" from the National Park Service.

Campgrounds
Apostle Islands Area Campground
½ mile south of Bayfield on Highway 13 & County J
715-779-5524

Big Bay State Park
Madeline Island
715-747-6425
Reservations must be made through Reserve America (reserveamerica.com) 888-947-2757

Big Bay Town Park
Madeline Island
1st come/1st served (Fee for use—
  payable at campground)

Buffalo Bay Campground and Marina
14669 Highway 13
Bayfield, WI 54814
Located in the Village of Red Cliff, 2 ½ miles north of Bayfield
715-779-3743

Dalrymple Campground
1 mile north of Bayfield on Highway 13
1st come/1st served (Fee for use—
  payable at campground)
Operated by City of Bayfield
cityofbayfield.com

Little Sand Bay Campground
715-779-5233
Operated by Town of Russell

Memorial Park
Washburn, WI
715-373-6174
Operated by Town of Washburn

Point Detour Campground
1st come/1st served (Fee for use—payable at
  campground). Operated by National Park Service.

West End Park
Washburn, WI
715-373-6174
Operated by Town of Washburn

Cruise Boats/Water Taxis/Ferry
Apostle Islands Cruise Service
City Dock
Bayfield, WI 54814
800-323-7619/715-779-3925
www.apostleislandscruises.com

Apostle Trawlers (Captain Jeff Janacek)
Island cruising
651-485-8989
apostletrawlers.com

Adventure Vacations
Water taxis and tours from Madeline Island
104 Middle Road
La Pointe, WI 54850
715-747-2100/866-910-0300
www.Adv-Vac.com

Nourse's Sport Fishing (Water taxi service also)
100 Yacht Club Drive, end of 3rd St.
Bayfield, WI 54814
866-819-4330/715-779-3253
www.noursesfishing.com

Madeline Island Ferry Line
Operates about every ½ hour during the day from
  both Bayfield and Madeline Island
715-747-2051
www.madferry.com

Fishing Charters

Angler's All (Captain Roger LaPenter)
2803 Lake Shore Drive East
Ashland, WI 54806
715-682-5754
anglersallwisconsin.com

Black Hawk Fishing Charters (Captain Ken Nourse)
86800 Betzold Road
Bayfield, WI 54814
800-779-3261
blackhawkcharters.com

Captain Craig's Lake Superior Guide Service
(Captain Craig Putchat)
1813 W, Bayfield St.
Washburn, WI 54891
outdoorallure.com

Dave's Fishing Charters (Captain Dave Sorenson)
PO Box 206
Ashland, WI 54806
715-682-3379
davesfishingcharters.com

Nourse's Sport Fishing (Captain Laurie Nourse)
100 Yacht Club Drive, end of 3rd St.
Bayfield, WI 54814
866-819-4330/715-779-3253
www.noursefishing.com

River Rock Charters (Captain Scott Bretting)
1200 West Lake Shore Drive
Ashland, WI 54806
715-682-3232/715-292-1085
www.riverrockinn.net

Roberta's Sport Fishing Charters (Captain Tony Rippel)
91950 Highway K
PO Box 841
Bayfield, WI 54814
715-779-5744/888-806-0944
www.robertascharters.com

Friends of the Apostle Islands National Lakeshore/Apostle Islands Historic Preservation Conservancy

Friends of the Apostle Islands National Lakeshore
PO Box 1574
Bayfield, WI 54814
715-779-3397 Ext. 444
friendsoftheapostleislands.org

Apostle Islands Historic Preservation Conservancy
Mr. Robert Mackreth
500 Woodland Drive
Washburn, WI 54891
715-373-0818
www.bobmackreth.com

Golf Courses
Apostle Highlands Golf Course
34745 Madeline Trail
Bayfield, WI 54814
715-779-5960/877-222-4053
1 mile south of Bayfield off Highway 13(County J)
www.golfbayfield.com

Chequamegon Bay Golf Course
Highway 137, west of Ashland
715-682-8004
www.golfashland.com

Madeline Island Golf Course
South of La Pointe
715-747-3212
www.madelineislandgolf.com

Hiking

National Park Service, *Hiker's Guide to Apostle Islands National Lakeshore*, Edited by Neil Howk, Asst. Chief of Resources Education, Apostle Islands National Lakeshore, Fort Washington: Eastern National, 2001.

McKinney, John, *The Joy of Hiking: Hiking the Trailmaster Way*, Berkeley: Wilderness Press, 2005.

Website describing hiking trails in the islands:
gorp.com/gorp/resource/us_ns/wi/hik_apo.htm

Kayaks/Canoes

Adventure Vacations-Madeline Island (kayaks)
104 Middle Road
La Pointe, WI 54850
715-747-2100/866-910-0300
www.Adv-Vac.com

Living Adventure Inc. (kayaks)
88260 State Highway 13
Bayfield WI 54814
715-779-9503/866-779-9503
www.livingadventure.com
Located 2 miles north of Bayfield in Red Cliff

Apostle Islands Kayaks-Madeline Island
715-747-3636
apostleislandskayaks.com

Wilderness Inquiry (kayaks)
33090 Little Sand Bay Rd.
Bayfield, WI 54814
800-728-0719/612-676-9400

Boreal Shores (kayaks)
222 Rittenhouse Avenue
Bayfield, WI 54814
(715)779-5500
borealshores.com

Trek & Trail Adventure Outfitters (kayaks)
7 Washington Ave
Bayfield, WI 54814
800-354-8735/715-779-3595

Bog Lake Outfitters
Canoe and rowboat rentals
Big Bay Town Park, Madeline Island
715-747-2685

Lighthouses
Strozk, Dave and Trapp, Nancy, *Lighthouses of the Apostle Islands,* Bayfield: 2001. Also available in VHS video format produced by Dave Strozk and Mike Pruett.

Lighthouse Celebration Cruises (early September)
PO Box 990
Bayfield, WI 54814
800-779-4487
lighthousecelebration.com

Keeper of the Light
19 Front Street
Bayfield, WI 54814
800-779-4487
keeperofthelight.net
This store stocks a variety of nautical and lighthouse merchandise.

Museums

Ashland Historical Society Museum
509 W. Main Street
Ashland, WI 54806
715-682-4911
ashlandhistory.com

Bayfield Heritage Center
30 N. Broad Street
Bayfield, WI 54814
715-779-5958
bayfieldheritage.org

Bayfield Maritime Museum
131 S. 1st Street
Bayfield, WI 54814
715-779-9919

Cornucopia Historic Green Shed Museum
Highway 13 at the Siskiwit Bay harbor
Cornucopia, WI 54827

Madeline Island Museum
226 Woods Ave.
La Pointe, WI 54850
715-747-2415
wisconsinhistory.org/madelineisland

Washburn Cultural Center
1 E. Bayfield Street (State Highway 13)
Washburn, WI 54891
715-373-5591

National Park Service
Apostle Islands National Lakeshore Headquarters
415 Washington Ave
Bayfield, WI 54814
715-779-3397
nps.gov/apis

Northern Great Lakes Visitor Center
29270 County Road G
Ashland, WI 54806
715-685-9983
NGLVC.org
Located on County Road G, ½ mile west of
 junction of US 2 and State Route 13, west of
 Ashland, WI

Sailboat Charters-Bareboat
Apostle Islands Yacht Charter Association
Madeline Island Yacht Club
800-821-3480/715-747-2983

Sailboats Inc.
100 Manypenny St.
Bayfield, WI 54814
800-826-7010 (reservations line)
715-779-3269
www.sailboats-inc.com

Superior Charters, Inc.
34475 Port Superior Rd
Bayfield, WI 54814
715-779-5124
SuperiorCharters.com

Sailboat Charters-Captained

Animaashi Sailing Co.
888-272-4548/715-779-5468
animaashi.com

Apostle Islands Yacht Charter Association
Madeline Island Yacht Club
800-821-3480/715-747-2983

Bayfield Charter Company
715-567-0112
bayfieldchartercompany.com

Catchun-Sun Charter
888-724-5494/715-779-3111
www.catchun-sunchartercompany.com

Dreamcatcher Sailing
800-682-1587/715-779-5561
wolfsongadventures.com/dreamcatcher/

Manitou Classic Sailing Charters
13 S. Second St. Unit #3
Bayfield, WI 54814
612-850-2981

Northern Breezes
Pike's Bay Marina
Bayfield, WI 54814
763-542-9707
NorthernBreezesSchool.com

Sailboats Inc
100 Manypenny St.
Bayfield, WI 54814
715-779-3269/800-826-7010 (reservations line)
www.sailboats-inc.com

Superior Charters, Inc.
34475 Port Superior Rd
Bayfield, WI 54814
715-779-5124
SuperiorCharters.com

Viking Charters, LLP
Bayfield, WI 54814
507-236-4415
captaindave@vikingcharters.net

ZaBreeNa
84196 Pike's Bay Road
Bayfield, WI 54814
651-336-7357

Sailing Schools
Apostle Islands Yacht Charter Association
Madeline Island Yacht Club
800-821-3480/715-747-2983

Northern Breezes
763-542-9707
NorthernBreezesSchool.com

North Coast Community Sailing
North Coast Sailing School
715-209-2352
northcoastcommunitysailing.org

Sailboats Inc
100 Manypenny St.
Bayfield, WI 54814
800-826-7010/715-779-3269   www.sailboats-inc.com

Superior Charters, Inc.
34475 Port Superior Rd
Bayfield, WI 54814
715-779-5124
SuperiorCharters.com

THANKS AND ACKNOWLEDGMENTS

James Harper

Scott Hafenscher

Wayne Hafenscher

Richard Jacobson

Stuart Richter

Christine Newman

Ronald and Paula Newman

Scott and Diane Newman

Paul and Donna Newman

Carol Swartz

James Thoreson

Ashland Chamber of Commerce

Northern Great Lakes Visitor Center—Exhibits

National Park Service personnel at the Apostle Islands National Lakeshore Center—Jim Nepstad and Julie Van Stappen

AUTHOR PROFILE

Lawrence Newman is the President of Silver Millennium Publications, Inc. and author of numerous books, including three about his favorite subject—the Apostle Islands, an archipelago of twenty two islands located off Wisconsin's northern shore in western Lake Superior, home of the Apostle Islands National Lakeshore, deemed the most pristine national park in the United States. He has also written books on other subjects, including self-publishing and quote compilations. In his prior life he was a Senior Vice President and Chief Financial Officer for Underwriters Laboratories, Inc. before he retired in 2001, after eighteen years with that public safety testing organization.

Anyone interested in pursuing the publication of his or her own book is welcome to contact him at silvermillpub@gmail.com. Books published by Silver Millennium Publications, Inc. can be viewed at Amazon.com and Barnesandnoble.com. Retailers' inquiries are also welcome.

www.ingramcontent.com/pod-product-compliance
Lightning Source LLC
Chambersburg PA
CBHW042321150426
43192CB00001B/14